FEB 0 5 ENT'D

D0463208

NASCAR
THE NEED FOR SPEED

Mike Johnstone

LERNER
SPORTS
AN IMPRINT OF LERNER PUBLISHING GROUP

CREDITS

First American edition published in 2002 by LernerSports

Original edition published 2001 by Franklin Watts

This book is available in two editions:
Library binding by LernerSports
Soft cover by First Avenue Editions
Imprints of Lerner Publishing Group
241 First Avenue North
Minneapolis, MN 55401 U.S.A.
Website address: www.lernerbooks.com

Picture credits: All photographs, including details, supplied by
Allsport UK Ltd. Front cover: top (Jamie Squire), middle (Yukio
Yoshimi), bottom (Craig Jones) Back cover: (Yukio Yoshimi) pp. 1
main (Craig Jones), 1 inset (Yukio Yoshimi), 2-3 main (David Taylor),
5 main (Jamie Squire), 5 inset (Craig Jones), 6 centre left (Jamie
Squire), 7 main (Robert Laberge), 8 bottom left and right (Robert
Laberge), 9 main (David Taylor), 10 bottom left (Jon Ferrey), 10-11
centre (Yukio Yoshimi), 11 main (David Taylor), 11 inset (David
Taylor), 12 bottom left (Jamie Squire) 13 main (Jamie Squire) 13
inset (Chris Stanford), 14 inset (Robert Laberge), 14-15 main
(Jamie Squire), 16 centre (Jonathan Ferrey), 16-17 main (David
Taylor), 18 bottom right (David Taylor), 19 main (Robert Laberge),
20 bottom (Jamie Squire), 21 main (Jamie Squire), 21 top right
(Robert Laberge), 23 main (Jamie Squire), 23 inset (Jon Ferrey), 24
bottom left (David Taylor), 25 main (Jamie Squire), 25 inset (Robert
Laberge), 26 bottom left (Robert Laberge), 27 main (David Taylor),
28 bottom left (David Taylor), 29 main (David Taylor)

Library of Congress Cataloging-in-Publication Data

Johnstone, Michael, 1946-
  NASCAR / by Michael Johnstone.
     p. cm. -- (The need for speed)
Includes index.
Summary: Describes some of the major races, cars, and key figures
connected with stock car racing sponsored by NASCAR.
  ISBN 0-8225-0389-1 (lib. bdg.)
  ISBN 0-8225-0392-1 (pbk.)
  1. Stock cars (Automobiles)--Juvenile literature. 2. Stock car
racing--Juvenile literature. [1. Stock car racing. 2. NASCAR
(Association)] I. Title. II. Series.
  TL236.28 .J64 2002
  796.72'0973--dc21   2001003469

Bound in the United States of America
  2 3 4 5 6 – OS – 07 06 05 04 03

CONTENTS

INTRODUCTION

If you have ever wanted to know what it feels like to drive some of the most exciting cars in the world, then The Need for Speed will show you.

It wasn't long after the automobile began to appear on the road that drivers started to race their vehicles, and the sport of car racing was born. The sport has now evolved into several branches, including stock-car racing—a competition between drivers in production models modified for the racetrack.

In the United States, stock-car racing contains so many different classes that almost anyone with a car can join in. At the highest level of the sport, drivers take the wheels of extremely tuned cars that cost millions of dollars to develop and maintain in race condition. Crowds of spectators flock to watch drivers roar around the track in pursuit of the biggest prize in stock-car racing—the Winston Cup—and the fortune in prize money and sponsorship deals that comes with it.

Stock-car racing in the United States is governed by NASCAR—the National Association for Stock Car Automobile Racing. This book focuses on the excitement of NASCAR racing—one of the fastest-growing sports in the United States!

Along with giving you a taste of the spectacles and thrills of NASCAR racing, we also give you the facts and figures behind some of these incredible machines and the tracks where they race. These are found in the Stat Files and Track Files, which look like this.

STAT FILE

CHEVROLET LUMINA

Wheelbase	110 in (279.5 cm)
Weight	3500 lb (1586 kg)
Brakes	Ventilated disc brakes
Engine	358 ci (5867 cc), ohv.1-4V, V-8, 700 hp
Transmission	Borg Warner Super T-10, floor-shift, four-speed manual

NASCAR

This organization was founded in 1947 by Bill France, a pioneer of the sport. France decided that stock-car racing needed "a little organization." NASCAR sanctioned its first race at Daytona Beach, Florida, the following year and has overseen the sport ever since.

NASCAR specifies which modifications allow the car to retain "stock" status within its class. The organization aims to have all cars raced in each class as equal as possible.

Fact Files give you slightly unusual, strange, or funny information.

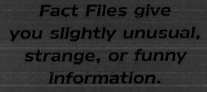

FACT FILE

Leading stock-car drivers have to be physically fit to cope with the demands of driving at such high speeds for long periods. Drivers work out in the gym every day, and many cycle long distances on mountain bikes.

In November 1895, J. Frank Duryea, driving a car he had made himself, won a race that started in Chicago, Illinois, and finished in Evanston, Illinois, 52.5 miles (84 kilometers) away. He took 10 hours to complete the course! As cars grew in popularity, mechanics started tinkering with them to make them go faster. In 1909 the first race to be billed "stock car" was held on 23 mi (36.8 km) of the streets of Long Island, New York.

By 1915 the sport moved off the road when a stock-car race was run on a specially built wooden track at the Chicago Speedway. But it was at a beach in Florida that stock-car racing really took off.

As cars developed, manufacturers were eager to see what speed they could reach. Someone, no one knows who, thought that the endless flat sands on Florida's Atlantic coast would be an ideal place to hold timed trials.

The competitive spirit soon took over, and within a few months impromptu races were being run. Cars roared northward along the beach at top speed, before slowing down to make a long turn off the sand onto Highway A1A—just 20 feet (6 meters) wide. There, the drivers put their feet down hard on the accelerator before braking and making a long, sweeping turn back onto the beach. One lap of the "track" was just under 4 mi (6.4 km). The beach was in Daytona—still regarded by stock-car enthusiasts as the birthplace of their sport!

Sponsorship

NASCAR stock-car racing is very expensive. Racing teams depend on big companies to provide funding. In return, the teams put sponsors' logos all over their cars so everyone at the track and watching on TV can see them. It's a highly visible form of advertising.

FACT FILE

Race Day

NASCAR races are held on oval-shaped tracks. The corners slope inward so that the cars can go around them at high speeds. The race always runs in a counterclockwise direction. The cars must be very tough, because in NASCAR it is acceptable for vehicles to collide. At the end of the race, many cars are badly dented. Some don't finish the race.

7

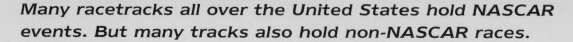

Many racetracks all over the United States hold NASCAR events. But many tracks also hold non-NASCAR races.

The premier circuits include Bristol Motor Speedway in Tennessee, nicknamed "The World's Fastest Half-Mile," with its track banked to 36 degrees to keep the cars from flying off. In Indiana, there's Brownstown Speedway, half the length of Bristol and banked to just 10 degrees. Brownstown is a great favorite with fans of Dirt Late Model racing. This sport became popular in the 1990s, when it was heavily featured on cable and satellite television.

Some tracks have large grandstands and lavish hospitality suites, where wealthy sponsors entertain their guests in style. On the other hand, there is Road Hog racing, where old Lincolns, Fords, and Chevrolets bang bumpers and spin off the track as their amateur drivers put them through their paces. Spectators here may be offered little more than a wooden seat on a grassy bank, with a hot dog stand nearby. Either way, it's a great day (or night) out.

For NASCAR events, thousands of fans cram the trackside stands to watch Jeff Gordon and other star drivers pit their skills against one another in lap after thrilling lap.

Pre-race parades give little hint of the thrills in store for spectators.

Each circuit has trackside pits where drivers refuel their cars.

The Winston Cup

The Winston Cup is the most coveted prize for the best stock-car drivers. The cup is sought in a series of races run over more than 20 U.S. tracks. NASCAR lays down strict rules to make sure that the cars of the Winston Cup contenders are as equal as possible. For example, drivers who weigh in at less than 160 pounds (72 kilograms) must add lead weights to their cars so that they gain no advantage from their lighter size!

FACT FILE

The Busch Grand National (BGN) Series

The BGN is sometimes called the Winston Cup's little brother. BGN cars are powered by the same V-8 engines as their bigger relatives but are not as highly tuned.

Busch cars have a 105-inch (267-centimeter) wheelbase—5 in (12.7 cm) less than Winston competitors. This makes a big difference in handling. Most of the stars of the Winston Cup, including Jeff Gordon, honed their race skills in the BGN series.

CHEVROLET

Chevrolet is one of the biggest names in NASCAR. A glance at the Winston Cup Roll of Honor shows that since 1957 Chevy drivers have won the biggest prize of stock-car racing 20 times, including six years in a row from 1993 to 1998.

In 1955 Chevrolet unveiled its 265 cubic-inch (4343 cubic-centimeter) small-block V-8 engine. It sent nearly every other engine design to the scrap heap. No other engine at the time could develop 180 horsepower at 4800 revolutions per minute with an 8:1 compression ratio and a four-barrel carburetor. Two years later, a car powered by an improved version reached 130 miles per hour (209 kilometers per hour) at Daytona Beach.

The 1960s saw Chevrolet sitting on the sidelines, but it came back in the 1970s. At that time, Cale Yarborough left Ford and took the wheel of a Chevrolet Laguna S-3. He pushed the car to the 153 mph (246 km/h) mark at Darlington, South Carolina. The late, great Dale Earnhardt's 1979-1980 Chevy Monte Carlo and Ernie Irvan's 1991 Lumina were worthy successors.

The 1990s saw the Chevrolet-driving trio of Dale Earnhardt, Terry Labonte, and Jeff Gordon winning again and again. The current Lumina is one of the fastest cars on the Winston Cup circuit with a possible top speed in excess of 200 mph (322 km/h).

STAT FILE

CHEVROLET LUMINA

Wheelbase	110 in (279.5 cm)
Weight	3500 lb (1586 kg)
Brakes	Ventilated disc brakes
Engine	358 ci (5867 cc), ohv.1-4V, V-8, 700 hp
Transmission	Borg Warner Super T-10, floor-shift, four-speed manual

DAYTONA

Whoever had the idea to hold timed trials at Daytona Beach probably had little idea of what they were starting. Daytona has become the most famous stock-car racetrack in the world. To many people, Daytona IS stock-car racing!

As cars increased their speed in the 1930s, timed trials moved from Daytona to the safer salt flats of Bonneville, Utah, but stock-car drivers decided to go on racing at Daytona. Their decision was backed by the American Automobile Association, which sanctioned a race there in 1936.

Louis Meyer won the race at the wheel of a 1934 Ford. He somehow managed to steer his car at high speed through the deep ruts that developed on the turns.

As more and more ruts formed in later races, drivers started to slide their cars around the bends with spectacular results. Some cars flipped over, while others lost springs, oil pans, and other parts.

More and more drivers headed for the beach at Daytona. Attracted by the prospect of thrills and spills, crowds of spectators followed.

FACT FILE

The Victory Lane

When Winston Cup races are over, the victors take their places in Daytona's Victory Lane.
The winners are added to a roll of honor that boasts the names of all the greats who have won at Daytona.

12

It's the Pits

When drivers need to refuel, they drive off the track into the pit lane. As soon as the car stops, a team of technicians gets to work. They put in more fuel, change the tires, and make any repairs as quickly as possible so that the driver can get back in the race.

History on Track

Daytona became the unofficial home of stock-car racing, and it was at Daytona Beach that Bill France founded NASCAR racing in 1947. As the sport grew in popularity, so did the nearby town. The track had to be continually relocated as new buildings and roads crowded the beach. Tired of this, France bought vacant land not far from Daytona Airport, announcing that he was going to build "the biggest, fastest, and longest track in the States." And that's what he did.

DAYTONA INTERNATIONAL SPEEDWAY

Every February, more than 165,000 fans cram the stands at Daytona to watch the Daytona 500, the inaugural race of the NASCAR calendar. It is also the culmination of Daytona's "February Speedweek"—seven days of racing that include the all-star "Bud Shoot-Out" for Winston Cup pole position winners of the previous year.

Later on in the year, at the beginning of July, the floodlit Pepsi 400 attracts capacity crowds. The race is literally one of the hottest in the Winston Cup calendar. The Florida heat can send the temperature on the track soaring to 125°F (52°C).

It was at Daytona, in 1976, that Richard Petty lost one of the most memorable races in Winston Cup history. Petty and his close rival David Pearson were neck and neck coming into the last lap. After touching a few times, they crashed hard and spun off the track. Somehow Pearson managed to keep his car running, got it back on track, and nursed it across the finish line to win!

Daytona USA, which opened in July 1996, is more than a racetrack. It's a 480-acre (194-hectare), multimillion dollar motorsports mecca with something for anyone interested in racing cars.

Hold That Power

NASCAR grew concerned that companies sponsoring Winston Cup teams encouraged their drivers to bunch together at dangerously high speeds during televised races at Daytona and at Talladega, Alabama. The organization decided to insist that cars at these tracks be fitted with carburetor restrictor plates that limit horsepower and therefore reduce speed.

STAT FILE

Daytona Trackfacts

Length	2.5 mi (4 km)
Width	40 ft (12.2 m)
Banking	31 degrees on the turns, 18 degrees on the tri-oval
Total frontstretch	3800 ft (1158 m)
Pit road	1600 ft (488 m) long, 50 ft (15.2 m) wide

FACT FILE

Qualifying Records	Driver	Speed	Date
WINSTON CUP (500)	B. Elliot	210.364 mph (338.548 km/h)	2.9.87
BUSCH GRAND NATIONAL	T. Houston	194.389 mph (312.839 km/h)	2.10.87
Race Records	Driver	Speed	Date
WINSTON CUP (400)	B. Allison	173.473 mph (279.178 km/h)	7.4.80
BUSCH GRAND NATIONAL	G. Bodine	157.137 mph (252.887 km/h)	2.19.85

For most stock-car racing enthusiasts around the world, the nearest track is a short distance away.

In the United States, there are stock-car racetracks all over the country from coast to coast and north to south. It's only possible to list a few in the pages of this book. Here's some info on four of the best.

ATLANTA MOTOR SPEEDWAY

First built in 1960 and modernized in the 1990s, Atlanta Motor Speedway in Hampton, Georgia, is very popular with fans of stock-car racing. The original 1.522-mi (2.449-km) oval track was relaid and extended to 1.54 mi (2.479 km). The banking is 24 degrees, making it a steep challenge for even the best drivers. Among them are Geoff Bodine, who lapped the track in 28.074 seconds, reaching 197.478 mph (317.812 km/h), and Bobby Labonte, who averaged a record 169.904 mph (273.434 km/h). They both reached these speeds during the same Winston Cup 500-mi (800-km) race in November 1997.

MICHIGAN SPEEDWAY

The designers of Daytona International Speedway were also the brains behind the track in Brooklyn, Michigan. Almost every seat in the grandstand offers a view of the entire 2-mi (3.2-km) track with its 18-degree banking on the turns.

The track is wide enough for three or sometimes four cars to race side by side at speeds approaching 200 mph (322 km/h). Dale Jarrett set the race record of 173.997 mph (280.013 km/h) in June 1999. Dale Earnhardt Jr. holds the qualifying record with a speed of 191.149 mph (301.616 km/h) in August 2000.

RICHMOND INTERNATIONAL RACEWAY

Stock-car racing has been held in Richmond, Virginia, since the 1940s, first on a dirt track that was 0.5 mi (0.805 km) long. This was paved in 1968. Twenty years later, the track was extended to 0.75 mi (1.2 km) and relaid in a D-shape.

Richmond is one of the most modern tracks on the Winston Cup circuit. Many races are held at night under lights. Jeff Gordon lapped Richmond in 21.344 seconds averaging 126.499 mph (203.575 km/h) in May 1999, which is still a record. And no one has managed to beat Dale Jarrett's 108.70 mph (174.936 km/h) race average which he achieved here in September 1997.

LOWE'S MOTOR SPEEDWAY

The track in Concord, North Carolina, is one of the largest outdoor sport stadiums in the southeastern United States. Seating 167,000 fans, it hosts three Winston Cup races each year, including the Coca-Cola 600 on Memorial Day. Lowe's owners were among the first to stage pre-race entertainment such as car, motorbike, and bus jumps. They were also the first to install floodlights and to stage night racing.

The track is 1.5 mi (2.4 km) long with 24-degree banking. Dale Earnhardt Jr. reached 186.034 mph (299.393 km/h) when he set the lap record of 29.027 seconds in May 2000. Jeff Gordon's average speed of 160.306 mph (257.988 km/h), set in October 1999, still stands as the race record.

PONTIAC

General Motors' Pontiac cars had their first NASCAR win in 1957. In 1962 Glenn "Fireball" Roberts and his fellow Pontiac drivers won 22 of that season's 55 Winston Cup races. Pontiac withdrew factory backing in 1963. Although Pontiacs still appeared at minor-league tracks all over the United States, they were out of the running in the Winston.

In 1981, however, Pontiac decided to come back to the NASCAR starting grid. Since then, drivers such as the legendary Richard Petty and Rusty Wallace have driven Pontiacs to victory in race after race, and it was in a Pontiac Grand Prix that Wallace won the Winston in 1989.

The current Pontiac Grand Prix was introduced in 1996, four years after Petty finished his record-breaking 200-victory career. The car is rounder and smoother than the long-nose models that marked Pontiac's return to the racetrack in the 1980s. It's a sleek, aerodynamic wonder, slipping through the wind like a hot knife through butter. The body is built of flat sheet metal stretched over fully fabricated tubular steel frames. Under the hood, there's an assortment of General Motors components.

The engine, built around a Chevrolet small-block, can produce 700 hp, which is enough to propel a race-tuned Grand Prix to over 200 mph (322 km/h). Chevrolet parts are used for the front suspension, and a Ford 9-in (22.9-cm) differential is mounted at the rear.

Screw-jack adjustable coil springs and four gas-charged shock absorbers are mounted, one on each wheel, to give the driver a smooth ride.

STAT FILE	
PONTIAC GRAND PRIX	
Wheelbase	110 in (279.4 cm)
Weight	3400 lb (1,542 kg)
Brakes	Ventilated disc brakes
Engine	358 ci (5867 cc), ohv·1-4V, V-8, 700 hp
Transmission	Borg Warner Super T-10, floor-shift, four-speed manual

Halfway between Roanoke, Virginia, and Greensboro, North Carolina, sits the only track from NASCAR's first year still to hold regular stock-car races.

Martinsville opened in 1947 and was laid as a dirt track in 1955. The circuit was paved in 1995 and sits at the center of a racing complex that covers 300 acres (121 hectares). It attracts race fans and competitors from all over the United States.

For days before each meeting, transporter trucks with cars chained securely to their backs jam the roads leading to the track. Before the racing starts, the drivers are introduced to the cheering fans in a well-organized pre-match ceremony with all the flair that one expects from a major U.S. sporting event.

At 0.526 mi (0.847 km) long, Martinsville is the shortest track on the NASCAR circuit. However, all the top drivers rate it as one of the best. The banking may not be the steepest, and the straights aren't long enough to really put your foot down and reach top speed, but no driver completes 500 laps at Martinsville without being thoroughly tested.

STAT FILE

Martinsville Trackfacts

Length	0.526 mi (0.847 km)
Banking	12 degrees
Total frontstretch	800 ft (244 m)
Total backstretch	800 ft (244 m)

FACT FILE

Qualifying Records—NASCAR WINSTON CUP

Driver	Speed	Date
T. Stewart	95.371 mph (153.485 km/h)	9.29.00

Race Records—NASCAR WINSTON CUP

Driver	Speed	Date
J. Gordon	82.223 mph (132.325 km/h)	8.22.96

BRISTOL

When Tennessee's Bristol Motor Speedway first opened in 1961, the track was exactly 0.5 mi (0.8047 km) long. Drivers quickly made it one of the speediest tracks on the NASCAR circuit, earning it the nickname "The World's Fastest Half-Mile."

At the opening race, 30,000 enthusiasts cheered Johnny Allen as he crossed the finishing line first. But his name doesn't feature in the record books. He was the relief driver for Jack Smith, who got the credit for winning Bristol's inaugural race.

Bristol has upgraded its track and spectator facilities over the past 40 years. In 1992 the track was repaved with concrete. The stands seat 135,000 fans around the extended track, whose original 22-degree banking was increased by 14 degrees. The banking makes for some exciting moments when a driver of the caliber of Rusty Wallace takes a bend at top speed with rivals hot on his tail.

Before a race at Bristol or any other NASCAR track, teams of technicians are hard at work under the hood, doing whatever they can to make sure that when the cars line up for the start they are race-tuned to perfection.

FACT FILE

Qualifying Records	Driver	Speed	Time	Date
NASCAR WINSTON CUP	S. Park	126.370 mph (203.373 km/h)	15.184 secs	3.24.00
BUSCH GRAND NATIONAL	J. Green	124.428 mph (200.247 km/h)	15.421 secs	3.24.00
Race Records	Driver	Speed	Date	
NASCAR WINSTON CUP	C. Glotzbach	101.074 mph (162.663 km/h)	7.11.71	
BUSCH GRAND NATIONAL	H. Gant	92.929 mph (149.555 km/h)	4.4.92	

STAT FILE

Bristol Trackfacts

Length	0.533 mi (0.857 km)
Banking	36 degrees

As the clock ticks away and the start gets nearer, teams make last-minute checks to guarantee that the cars are in peak condition for the race to come.

23

DRIVERS

In the United States, top stock-car drivers are celebrities with their own websites and fan clubs. Drivers such as Jeff Gordon and Bobby Labonte are household names.

Richard Petty, the all-time great Winston Cup race winner who drove the Victory Lane 200 times before he retired in 1992, is a name known to millions of Americans coast to coast. His son, Kyle, and late grandson, Adam, have also taken the driver's seat. The Petty name is destined to be remembered for years to come.

As top NASCAR drivers, the Pettys know that even though their names are well known, they are still part of a team. It's no good being the best driver in the world if your car is going to break down at the first bend.

FACT FILE

Leading stock-car drivers have to be physically fit to cope with the demands of driving at such high speeds for long periods. Drivers work out in the gym every day, and many cycle long distances on mountain bikes.

They also need experience. It helps if racing is a family tradition, but all the great drivers have learned their craft in the lower ranks of stock-car racing before hitting the Winston Cup trail. Starting young is a great advantage. Jeff Gordon, for instance, was putting sprint cars through their paces when he was 13.

Davey Allison, whose career was cut short when he was killed in a helicopter crash in 1993, was even younger when he started his racing career. He began by tinkering with engines at the family's race shop when he was just 12!

A sad loss

Dale Earnhardt was a youngster when he took the wheel in the early 1970s. He went on to win 76 NASCAR races and seven Winston Cups. His career came to a tragic end at the Daytona 500 in 2001. Coming into the last bend of the last lap, his car hit a wall and he was killed instantly. Sitting in third place, he is thought to have been trying to prevent cars behind him from passing the driver in second place—his son, Dale Jr.

Dale Earnhardt's famous number 3.

NASCAR WINSTON CUP CHAMPIONS 1991-2000

1991	Dale Earnhardt,	Chevy
1992	Alan Kulwicki,	Ford
1993	Dale Earnhardt,	Chevy
1994	Dale Earnhardt,	Chevy
1995	Jeff Gordon,	Chevy
1996	Terry Labonte,	Chevy
1997	Jeff Gordon,	Chevy
1998	Jeff Gordon,	Chevy
1999	Dale Jarrett,	Ford
2000	Bobby Labonte,	Pontiac

INDIANAPOLIS

The track in Indianapolis, Indiana, is best known as the home of the famous Indy 500, "the world's greatest race," first run in 1911. NASCAR ran its first Winston Cup series event here in 1994, and it has been a firm favorite ever since.

Shortly after the track opened in 1909, the original crushed-stone-and-tar track surface started to crack. It was repaved with over 3.2 million bricks and has been known as "The Brickyard" ever since. One strip of the old brick remains visible, marking the start/finish line.

The first NASCAR race was won by local hero Jeff Gordon, who was cheered on by a crowd of 350,000, the largest crowd ever to watch a Winston Cup race. Other drivers to have won the "Brickyard 400" cup are Dale Jarrett, Dale Earnhardt, and Ricky Rudd.

Several noticeable changes helped accommodate NASCAR's arrival in Indianapolis. Although the fastest stock cars are slower than the monsters that compete in the Indy 500, crashes are more common in stock-car racing. The outer and inner crash walls had to be widened to contain the cars in case of an accident. Also, the circuit's famous scoreboard tower was enlarged to fit the names of the Winston Cup's 40 competitors—seven more than Indy car races.

The track in Indianapolis is not steeply banked but is among the fastest tracks in the world. This is because of the added straights between turns one and two and turns three and four.

Crowds hold their breath when crashes happen in NASCAR racing.

STAT FILE

Indianapolis Trackfacts

Length	2.5 mi (4 km)
Banking	12 degrees on turns

FACT FILE

Qualifying Records	Driver	Speed	Date
WINSTON CUP	B. Bodine	181.072 mph (291.407 km/h)	8.4.00
Race Records	Driver	Speed	Date
WINSTON CUP	B. Labonte	155.912 mph (250.916 km/h)	8.5.00

27

The old speedsters of the 1920s were usually Ford Model As with factory body parts, but they had modified engines and chassis. Ford has been at the heart of stock-car racing ever since.

A glance through the history books reveals models such as Tom Young's 1938 Ford Coupe (for which he paid $3.00 but came out ahead when he found $8.00 under the floor mat); Chris Turner and his "Purple Hog;" the Holman and Moody Galaxies of the 1960s; the Torino Talladegas of the 1960s and 1970s; and the Thunderbird.

Recent Thunderbirds are among the sleekest stock cars built. Countless hours on the drawing board and in the wind-tunnel test track have produced a car with smooth, rounded edges, a perfectly angled windshield, and a sloping roof line that slips smoothly around the circuit.

Ford's engine, restricted in competition to 550 hp, can produce up to 750 hp.

Ford had no Winston Cup champions after 1992, when Alan Kulwicki took the crown. With high-ranking drivers and a car the caliber of the current Thunderbird, Ford only needed to bide its time until it won. In 1999 Dale Jarrett duly obliged.

STAT FILE

FORD THUNDERBIRD

Wheelbase	110 in (279.5 cm)
Weight	3400 lb (1542 kg)
Brakes	Ventilated disc brakes
Engine	358 ci (5867 cc), ohv.1-4V, V-8, 700 hp
Transmission	Borg Warner Super T-10, floor-shift, four-speed manual.

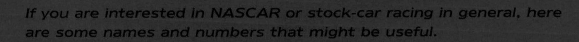

If you are interested in NASCAR or stock-car racing in general, here are some names and numbers that might be useful.

UNITED STATES

American Motor Racing Association
334 North 10th Street
Coshocton, Ohio 43812
email: doneverhart@hotmail.com
website: www.amramodified.com

Busch All-Star Series
NASCAR
P.O. Box 2875
Daytona Beach, Florida 32120
email: publicrelations@nascar.com
website: www.nascar.com

International Motor Contest Association (IMCA)
P.O. Box 921
Vinton, Iowa 52349
email: raceimca@aol.com
website: www.imca.com

NASCAR
P.O. Box 2875
Daytona Beach, Florida 32120
email: publicrelations@nascar.com
website: www.nascar.com

CANADA

Canadian Stock Car Auto Racing Association (CASCAR)
9763 Gledon Drive
Komoka, Ontario MOL 1RO
email: racing@cascar.ca
website: www.cascar.ca

TECHNICAL TERMS

backstretch: the straight length of a racetrack farthest from the finish line

banking: the angle at which the outer edge of a track slopes upward

carburetor: a device that controls the mixing of gasoline and air in an engine

chassis: the supporting structure or frame of a car

circuit: a track, sometimes surfaced, around which cars race

cockpit: the driving compartment of a racing car

cubic inches (ci): the measure of an engine's size

differential: a mechanism that allows the driving wheels to turn at different speeds

engine: a machine inside a car that turns the wheels and makes the car move

frontstretch: the long straight section of a racetrack where drivers cross the finish line

gear: the device that allows the driver to control the speed at which the engine is working

horsepower (hp): a measure of an engine's power; the greater the horsepower, the faster the car

pit: an area at the side of a racetrack where cars go to be refueled, have their tires changed, and be repaired

pole position: the best position at the start of a race

revolutions per minute (rpm): the rate at which an engine works

shock absorber: a part of a car's suspension system

sponsorship: money given to a racing team by a company that wants to gain publicity from the team's success

timed trial: a speed test where cars are timed over a specified distance

transmission: a car's gear system

V-8: an engine that has 2 banks of 4 cylinders each (8 total)

wheelbase: the distance between the front and rear axles of a car